SECURING THE B.A.G.

(Big Audacious Goals)

Cami Barnes

authorHOUSE®

AuthorHouse™
1663 Liberty Drive
Bloomington, IN 47403
www.authorhouse.com
Phone: 833-262-8899

Published by AuthorHouse 02/27/2023

ISBN: 979-8-8230-0194-6 (sc)
ISBN: 979-8-8230-0193-9 (hc)
ISBN: 979-8-8230-0195-3 (e)

Library of Congress Control Number: 2023903541

Print information available on the last page.

Contents

(Cami Barnes, January 2023, photo credit:

Dream Lens Photography)

Note to the Dreamers & Doers

I could assume that if you've decided to purchase this book, you are a part of my tribe. Daring to dream is one of your best qualities, you're creative, imaginative and from time to time you experience feelings of being unsettled in your current circumstances. Always thinking of what you can do next, ready to strive for the next bigger, greater challenge. It's also entirely possible that you aren't a part of the type A, perfectionist tribe which is fine. Maybe you have great ideas, but you've been feeling stuck and find yourself continuing to procrastinate about making the decision to act on some of those ventures. No matter which category you fall into, your feelings & beliefs are valid. This text is as much a guide as it is a benchmark for measuring success. I intend to share some of my journey and helpful tools for overcoming the pitfalls that can and will challenge you as you work towards your own version of success. I use the acronym "B.A.G." as a buzz word in the title but also because it's fitting. People use the phrase "securing the bag" as a way to convey getting paid or becoming financially secure, with heavy emphasis on obtaining money. There's also a phrase "getting" or "chasing" a bag, which infers a determination about obtaining money. I would like to flip that line of thinking on its head here and suggest securing or chasing your B.A.G. (Big Audacious Goals) because you will find fulfilment in your accomplishments and the money will flow to you as a result. Being primarily focused on money sounds good in theory, especially to people who have never had much of it. But society has shown us that even though money can buy things for short term happiness, the money alone doesn't seem to be enough if you don't find fulfilment in your life once you have it. There are millionaires and billionaires who have committed suicide, struggling to find genuine romantic partners & connections. As I talk about goals and manifesting your vision…not all of the focus will be on how that pertains to your career. There are other areas of your life that deserve as much attention as your professional life because you are a whole…entire person. If you are audacious enough to set big goals, be introspective enough to visualize what your ideal life looks like and include those goals in your plan as well.

(Cami as a baby, 1984)

Chapter 1

Recognizing Your Greatness

"Great spirits have always encountered violent
opposition from mediocre minds."

-Albert Einstein

All of the greatest superhero stories begin with an
unassuming person, encountering all manner of challenges on their
journey to becoming who they were meant to be. The heroes of
these stories are often mistreated, underestimated, they encounter
various life and personal obstacles which sets the foundation for
their stories. That build up to the catalyst serves an important
purpose for the audience, it's meant to help us understand the
hero's perspective on things as the story develops. It gives us a
lens through which to view the hero's experiences and it pulls us
in emotionally so that we are vested in the things that happen next
for the character. An additional purpose that the negative things
happening on the hero's journey serves, is to illicit excitement and
feelings of triumph once that character recognizes who they are

really meant to be as they harness their powers. Fulfilling their destiny.

Our lives are no different than this example I've provided. Think, for a moment, about your own life and the lives of other people who are wildly successful. Oprah, for instance, is easily one of the most successful women in media. She's a self-made billionaire who came from a life of poverty and child sexual abuse. She was born to a teen mother, raised in rural Mississippi without indoor plumbing, failed by every adult who didn't protect her as a child and battling the emotional issues that came along with trauma and abandonment. Her journey towards becoming the Oprah Winfrey that society celebrates today was fraught with so many things that could have easily prevented her from surviving. Yet she overcame every challenge heaped upon her to become a person who is very different than those who knew her back then would have ever expected. Let's ask ourselves and think about what the key to that success was? What separates the "Oprahs" from those of us who have backgrounds littered with pain and trauma but can't seem to move forward? The answer is mindset. There are some of us who, no matter what happens to us, no matter what we've survived, we are determined to elevate our lives and be everything that the naysayers said we couldn't be. So, to you, I say, tap in to that. The idea that you too can be successful, whatever your version of success is, you have the ability to attain it. It all starts with believing it and holding on to that belief fiercely. Don't allow any outside influence or person to shake that belief, allow it to become an essential part of your being, soak it in to your bone marrow so that it's there and permanent.

Like you, and others, I know all too well what it's like to encounter outside influences, challenges, barriers, traumas that are meant to stamp out your light. I spent more than half of my life not knowing my worth or value, due to being told that I would never be anything special. I grew up being called every foul name you can think of, with the maltreatment coming from various sources. I was extremely quiet, had low self-esteem, survived multiple layers of trauma including but not limited to having sexually inappropriate behaviors directed towards me, witnessing domestic violence, emotional abuse and being bullied in school. I was told by a high school teacher that I'd grow up to be a welfare recipient. I was so used to maltreatment that I found it difficult to distinguish that norm from the kind of treatment I should expect for myself. These experiences culminated in me wanting to escape, I was seeking something that I felt I never had. Deciding by the time I was 16

that the answer to all of my problems was to move out and have my

own family by the time I was 18 (the soonest I could legally do it).

Flawed thinking for sure, but it made sense in my teenaged, trauma

influenced mind. I did it. I became a teen mom (second generation)

and wife immediately after I graduated from high school. And by

the time I graduated from high school, five months pregnant with

my eldest daughter I'd attempted suicide twice… once at thirteen

and once at sixteen. What I wanted was true love, unconditional

and a family of my own that I could create and pour my own

love into, but my rush to do this and my intentions were always

hampered by that cloud of not knowing my worth. Consequently,

the maltreatment continued even after I'd created my little family,

as little more than a child myself, thinking that if I could just love

this person or that person enough, I'd be loved in the way I needed

to be. I had two children by the time I was twenty-two, I bounced

from abusive relationship to abusive relationship, experiencing

varying degrees of maltreatment, emotional abuse, physical abuse,

being raped twice, and nearly killed. Yet, despite all of these things

there was something on the inside of me that refused to believe that

I wasn't capable of great things.

Throughout my life, no matter how many times I was called stupid, there was always evidence to the contrary. There's so much irony in that particular insult when I was actually classified as exceptional academically. I would have had the opportunity to skip the first grade were it not for the fact that I was already the youngest in all of my classes due to a late birthday and starting school early. I was four years old entering kindergarten and my mother felt I wasn't emotionally mature enough to skip a grade even though I was displaying higher than average intelligence. In the sixth grade, I tested and was accepted to a combined middle/ high school for academically advanced children, which I graduated from (in spite of being pregnant). So, there were always battling beliefs warring in my brain and hovering throughout the chaos that was my life. Deep down I always knew I was intelligent and that was the one thing nobody could ever take away from me. I always intended to go to college, and had goals of achieving some level of success, even if I didn't always know what steps to take to make those things a reality.

As I worked full time, with two young children, to put myself through college I continued to face challenges and barriers. There were many late nights, staying up after my household was asleep to study and complete assignments. Tears of frustration with the difficulties of finding a day care center that was willing to administer medication to my asthmatic toddler. Finding reliable support, I had an agreement with someone who was supposed to pick my children up from day-care and keep them until I got off from work, but I'd receive calls that my children weren't picked up and would have to zip across town to get them myself. Days of standing in the cold to donate plasma to afford the things that my children needed. Hearing distant gun shots in the neighborhood, and not knowing for sure how distant they were so I'd grab my daughters and lie down on the floor to avoid any potential stray bullets. This was the struggle life, combined with my trauma history and a few men who tried throw me off course...taking advantage of an ever-present love of love. In the midst of it all, the tears, the frustration, the sleepless nights, living in a less than ideal neighborhood because it's what I could afford at the time...it was temporary. I was determined to keep going and improve my station in life for myself and my children.

Now that we've established the foundation...where, you might ask, is the catalyst? What was it that sparked a change in my mindset, allowing me to fully recognize that I was more than worthy? What helped me to heal, harness my power and begin

using my voice? It happened near the end of my undergraduate

education at Wright State University. Over time I'd become a

version of myself that would just do, and do, pushing forward was a

way of coping with the unaddressed trauma and hurt that I carried.

My sleepless nights weren't just a conscious decision to stay awake

to complete my coursework, the sleepless nights also included vivid

nightmares and panic attacks. I suppressed so much during the

daytime hours by doing...that the trauma reared its ugly head in

my subconscious. It all came to a head as I was taking a Women's

Studies course, and the topic for two weeks was "Violence Against

Women". As my college professor lectured about assaults, and

abuse it was like a dam broke and the floodgates opened. I sat in

class with tears, pouring down my face. It was there that I came

to terms with the things I'd survived, and I realized that there was

nothing I did to deserve those things. After class, my professor

pulled me aside and told me about a group she ran on campus

called "Women of Strength", it was a network of sexual assault

and domestic violence survivors who met to empower and support

one another and used their voices to speak out at awareness events

on campus and in the community. I found my healing, my power and my voice by acknowledging my traumas and speaking out in support of others. I started therapy and began working on rebuilding myself from the inside as I continued to accomplish the goals, I had to improve my station in life.

Speaking out was outside of my comfort zone, acknowledging the things that happened to me made them real, I could no longer suppress them and ignore the trauma by focusing on everything else. There were also fears tied to speaking that stemmed from being so quiet growing up, lacking confidence, wondering if what I had to say would really matter to anyone. But there is greatness on the other side of the discomfort that comes from pushing yourself to do things, outside of your norm, in the pursuit of personal growth. Recognizing my worth, and value was a game changer for me. It became a snowball effect which culminated in me seeking more and more ways to grow and empower other people. Speaking and empowerment has become central to who I am. Pushing myself to accomplish goals that nobody who knew that younger version of me would expect. It became a force within me, driving me, proving who I am to myself and to those who doubted me. All while helping others along the way.

(Cami & Daughters, Wright State University

Commencement Ceremony Spring 2012)

Chapter 2
The B.A.G.

"The most difficult thing is the decision to
act; the rest is merely tenacity."

-Amelia Earhart

In order to unlock new levels of success, you have to
be ambitious enough to think of new goals to accomplish and
audacious enough to believe you can. The phrase "Big Hairy
Audacious Goal" was coined by Jim Collins in his book "Built to
Last" but for our purposes I've used the acronym, B.A.G. instead,
Big Audacious Goal. Jim Collins' B.H.A.G. is geared towards
companies and is meant to galvanize companies and corporations
to achieve incredible results. My acronym is similar in the way that
it's meant to motivate but it's geared towards individuals as a way
to push them past their own limiting beliefs. In this text, B.A.G.
is much more fitting, it serves its purpose, ties in with my book
title and breathes a fresh perspective onto the slang term "securing
the bag".

Think of the biggest goal you can for yourself. A goal so

big that it seems a bit scary to consider and makes you question whether you're qualified or capable of achieving it. Have you found it? The best thing you can do to grow professionally is to push yourself past those limits that have kept you complacent and stagnant. By making a decision to do something different, you've already taken the first step towards walking in your greatness. Nothing grows in the comfort zone, it feels safe, it doesn't require much of you but it's where dreams go to die.

Before I became a full-time entrepreneur, I had a career in human resources working for a health department which covered multiple Atlanta area counties in the state of Georgia. There's job security in state jobs which boast great benefits, health, vision, dental, life, 401K, and a pension if you stay long enough to become "vested". I liked the organization, the atmosphere, and the people even though the salary was low…as is the norm for the public sector. I had job security… a "good job" by many people's standards, benefits and a steady, predictable paycheck coming in every two weeks. I never did feel fulfilled in that role though I tried for four years, doing everything in my power to utilize my skills and strengths to enrich what felt like a cozy little glass box. I joined every committee, I volunteered for special events and

projects, I even taught a free fitness class (free because they refused
to pay me any additional money or allow me to charge) for the
employees. That little glass box just continued to get tighter around
me. Then one day I decided to start my non-profit organization,
Safe Space Property Management Inc, expecting it to be the
missing piece to help me to feel as though I was walking in my
purpose.

My non-profit organization, affectionately known as "Safe
Space ATL" is a 501c3 tax exempt charity that provides supportive
services to domestic violence survivors and their children. The
idea for Safe Space was born during the most tumultuous time
of my life, when I took my daughters and fled a domestically
violent relationship. It was in those moments that I realized how
important it was for abuse victims to have support, as I moved in
with a close friend. She allowed me and my children to live with
her until I could save enough money to get another place for us.
The seed was planted during that time, but it took several years to
come to fruition, mostly because it never seemed like the perfect
time to do it and partly because in that timeframe I graduated
from college and rebuilt my life. But while I was working as a
Human Resources Generalist/Recruiter for the health department

I felt a strong desire to just do it. I felt like I heard God's voice telling me to do it and no matter how I protested, the voice became louder until I was obedient and did it. I had never registered a business before or run a non-profit organization but what I lacked in knowledge I made up for with the passion that I had for that demographic. I knew that I wanted to provide transitional housing to domestic violence survivors and their children. I didn't have all of the pieces or the answers for how I would do that. But I registered the business, domain, website and began investing in additional business needs like marketing materials as I created the framework for what I wanted the organization to represent. There are so many things that I learned along the way, mistakes that I made, people I trusted that I shouldn't have but it was all a part of the process. One thing I didn't realize when I initially registered Safe Space is that in order to apply and attain 501c3 status with the IRS, the organization structure had to be an Inc instead of an LLC. So a few months after registering the business with the state and working to build the foundation for the organization I had to re-register Safe Space Property Management as an Inc. Being designated as a 501c3 would open up more opportunities for grant funding which I discovered as I worked to figure out ways to fund services that I wanted to provide to survivor families in the community. As with most start-up businesses and organizations I funded nearly everything initially out of my own pocket, and over time began planning ways to fundraise and receive donations for my cause. I also learned prior to applying for 501c3 status as a non-profit that the organization had to have board members, so I set out to find two women with a similar passion for Safe Space's mission and vision. I eventually grew my board of directors to five amazing women who all have personal connections to domestic violence and at the time of the writing of this book, we've provided supportive services to survivors in the community for the past four years.

Did I mention that I built my non-profit organization during my last two years working full time for the health department? It was a challenge providing services to the community including but not limited to short term emergency shelter, case management, fitness classes, monetary donations, furniture & household item donations, childcare assistance and funds for barrier removal while trying to keep what I was doing under wraps from my employer. This became especially difficult as Safe Space started to receive media attention from local news entities. People at work began coming up to me to say that they saw me on the news discussing our Annual Holiday Toy Drive, or they saw me in the newspaper talking about my organization. Those who approached me were all very supportive and made no attempts to bring what I was doing to the attention of my manager, the HR Director. There were co-workers who were fiercely loyal to me and my vision for my little organization. They attended fundraising events, donated to our cause, passed out my business cards to patients who came into the health department that showed signs of abuse or expressed a need for help. It felt good to be able to do my job well in HR, juggle all of the additional tasks I'd taken on in that role and be able to provide services to the community through Safe Space. But I knew it was only a matter of time before my manager would discover my alternate identity as the Founder & Executive Director of a small org that was making a big impact. I felt like a female version of Clark Kent, in the comic Super Man, carefully crafting the image of a quiet, unassuming, overlooked professional while literally being a lifeline for those in need. It was mildly amusing, because I've always viewed being underestimated as a superpower that I'd mastered. One of the best things about being in a position where people don't realize how great you are is the shock and awe that ensues when they do.

I fully intended to leave the health department once I'd attained enough funding to work Safe Space full time. The business structure for the org didn't allow a way for me to be paid a salary as Executive Director and my employment wages provided a small cushion to support operational costs and our services in addition to any funding we brought in through fundraising. So I continued on in my HR role, the small but steady pay check, the connections I made with the employees I was able to help daily, along with my alternate identity with Safe Space kept me just comfortable enough to not leave. All of that changed drastically with a series of events that included a global virus pandemic, and a new baby.

In late 2019, my husband and I decided to have a baby. Husband??? Yes, after rebuilding my life I'd finally remarried, to a wonderful man who had four children of his own. We were essentially the black "Brady Bunch" with six kids between us, his four and my two. He tried for years to get me to agree to having a child with him, but I made the decision after my youngest daughter that I wouldn't have anymore, for a variety of reasons and then... fast forward to 14 years after having her I was open to the idea.

Back when I was twenty-two years old (2005), I was in

an abusive relationship, with a person who used pregnancy as a weapon, on me and on the other women he had children by. It was a weapon meant to be a barrier to my leaving him, being wanted by anyone else, and to discourage professional growth. He got me one time, deliberately getting me pregnant by sabotaging my birth control so I made sure that wouldn't happen again. I got my tubes tied and decided that no man would ever be able to trap me or use my body against me again.

I'll admit that during the early years of my relationship with my (now) husband, it was trust issues that prevented me from being open to the possibility of having another child. But in late 2019 that changed, I'm not sure exactly what caused the shift but similar to the divine intervention that pushed me to create my non-profit org, I felt and heard God's voice telling me to do it. At the time, my husband and I had been together for four years, and married for one year, when I broached the subject of us having a baby together. He, of course, was overjoyed and we began the challenging, medically assisted process of conceiving our son. As we were going through the process the world began to discuss this new virus that was impacting certain countries but hadn't made it to the United States. The "Coronavirus", a mysterious illness that was spreading, making people seriously ill and killing many. And then it happened, we were pregnant, and shortly after that confirmation there were confirmed cases of the Coronavirus in the United States and in the state of Georgia.

Working at the health department gave me a unique view and insight into the global virus pandemic that was unfolding as the world shut down, everyone was forced to work from home, and I was included on weekly Zoom meetings about the rising cases. As the world learned more about the virus there was an increased need for Coronavirus testing, which started being called Covid 19. Many of our staff at the health department were front line workers, and I, as the only recruiter for that district was tasked with recruiting to fill dozens of positions for nursing staff, testing site workers, and contact tracers.

Throughout my pregnancy there was a fear of the virus and encountering people who were infected with it. I also learned during those first few months of the pandemic how much I loved working from home. It wasn't just the safety of it, but I felt at peace, it brought me closer to my family and I felt more productive being able to work with less interruptions. But eventually a decision was made to start bringing staff back into the offices. I made the decision then that I needed to find a recruiter role that allowed me to work from home and planned to begin applying for opportunities during my maternity leave. I knew that my desire to work from home would only increase as my concern for my family's health and not wanting to leave my new baby became a reality.

During my leave I applied for hundreds of remote work recruiter roles, and I didn't get any offers, so I begrudgingly went back in to work, somewhat satisfied with being able to telework two days per week. And the pandemic raged on, with Covid 19 cases increasing and decreasing, millions of people hospitalized and dying. I continued applying for fully remote work and interviewed for what I thought was my dream job only to not get an offer. I was devastated but I prayed about it and resigned myself to the fact that there must have been a reason why I didn't get that job. The answer came from an unexpected place. On a reality show I was watching there was a man who was running his own recruitment and staffing agency. I thought to myself, I can do that! I have the skill set; I have the workforce development & recruitment background and that would be the perfect answer to this conundrum of needing a work from home recruitment role. It was in that moment that I made the decision to start my own agency, I began the process of preparing, took a course that provided me with the basics along with the contract templates I needed. And I prayed and told God that I needed a certain amount of money saved to quit my job and work my agency full time. And through a wacky combination of fortunate circumstances, I attained the exact amount of money I prayed for and said I needed. I'd started my agency, ExecuThrive Staffing LLC, and began building the foundation for my business, building my client base and securing my first direct hire recruitment contract. Even then, having attained the savings amount I felt comfortable with and landing a contract, I was hesitant to leave my job at the health department. The "what ifs" began to take over, but I typed up my resignation letter anyway. A wave of anxiety flooded over me, I sent the resignation letter anyway, all while one of my favorite quotes played over and over in my mind, "Do the scary thing first and get scared later." (Lemony Snicket).

Pushing past the fear that kept me complacent, making less money than what I deserved, feeling unfulfilled, and having to stifle my greatness is what unlocked a new level for me and my family. I was audacious enough to believe I had the ability to create this opportunity for myself. I was brave enough to smash that comfy but tiny glass box I felt I was in, and I was determined enough to keep pressing forward through the ups and downs of being a full-time entrepreneur, building a business brick by brick.

(Will & Cami Barnes, wedding reception September 2018)

Chapter 3
Pushing Past Limiting Beliefs

"It always seems impossible until it's done."

-Nelson Mandela

It can be challenging to hold steadfast to your knowledge of self as you encounter people on your path who try to heap their expectations and labels onto you. Even the most stubborn among us (raises hand) can have moments when we falter and allow negativity to seep into our subconscious. This is particularly difficult when you have a trauma history or other socioeconomic, racial, religious, cultural or gender disparities working against you. Society can make us feel less than, directly and indirectly. No matter how confident you are in your identity and your skills you may have moments where you second guess yourself. The key is to not allow those thoughts to hinder you from progressing forward. When you find yourself stuck in a negative thought loop, break the loop by swapping those thoughts and words with positive affirmations. What you see and hear can make a world of difference in your mindset. Surround yourself with great thinkers, innovators, and go getters. Being tapped into that energy, that motivated, creative, ambitious energy will help you to operate from that space as well.

I don't know that I've ever had limiting beliefs per se, even amid being emotionally abused, belittled and encountering micro-aggressions. I've always known I was capable of great things. But one thing I have experienced and continue to experience are bouts of imposter syndrome, I'm also prone to anxiety. As I've made strides towards becoming my version of successful, I'm completely confident until just before I'm about to speak or be interviewed. My mind goes into overdrive analyzing what people must be thinking of me. Do they see me as credible? Do they see me as worthy of being where I am? Are my words connecting and making an impact on the listener? And occasionally it's the comparison. Wow, "so and so" is so accomplished, am I at the level of being mentioned in the same sentence, to be listed on the same event program? But when this happens, I cut off the negative thought loop and reiterate the things I know to be true about myself. I highly recommend this strategy for high achievers who battle with imposter syndrome. Your thoughts can't argue with the facts. So, discredit the negative thoughts by listing out your accomplishments and remind yourself that you do have the skill set, you do have the expertise and you are who, deep down, you know yourself to be. For me and the Christian members of my tribe…you are who God says you are. Non-religious people are as welcome in my tribe and in my space as those who share my beliefs, so I'll never exclude you just know that much of my perspective on tenacity comes from being rooted in who I am and who God says I am. In my life and on my journey, God is the source of my strength, the renewing of my mind, and my place of peace. When I feel myself getting overwhelmed, stressed, upset and as I discredit any negative thoughts, I drown those thoughts out with positive affirmations and prayer. Non-religious people can use a similar strategy with discrediting the negative thoughts, positive affirmations, and meditation on those positive words. Either way it's disconnecting with anything negative and plugging in to a positive energy source.

Another tool and a great skill to have is the ability to positively reframe, it's an excellent coping technique that works in conjunction with cutting off negative thoughts. Being able to do this, focusing on the solutions instead of the problem is a way to re-center your thoughts and act towards changing the situation you're in. Feeling stuck on the problem does nothing but put you in a victim mindset, there's no action behind it and no real progress. When challenges and delays arise, don't ask yourself why is this happening to me, instead, ask yourself what is this trying to teach me? Identify that, come to terms with it, take the lesson and keep moving forward. Another spin on the positive reframe is flipping any negative traits or characteristics into a strength.

(Cami Barnes, October 2020, photo credit:

J. Sabastian Photography)

Chapter 4
Slaying Giants

"The best revenge is massive success."

-Frank Sinatra

Do you remember the story of "David & Goliath"? It's a bible story and one that's been used in popular culture to represent the underdog. The simplified version of the story is about a young boy who believed he could defeat the giant, Goliath. Nobody around him believed he could do it, and likely thought he was foolish for believing he could and out of his mind for being willing to try. To top it off, he rejected the armor that was offered to him for protection, choosing as his weapons of choice his faith, a sling shot and a few stones. Can you visualize this scenario playing out? Based on how things were going for the soldiers being continually defeated by Goliath, it must have seemed illogical for a young boy to be audacious enough to think he could make an impact on the situation. But he did it. Nobody believed he could, they counted him out, but he proved them all wrong. Anyone who's ever felt like the underdog can relate to David, I know I can. It can be annoying and discouraging when the people around you don't seem to believe in your capabilities, but just like in other scenarios I've described in this text, I challenge you to flip that around. Being underestimated is my favorite place to be in, simply because I take great satisfaction in proving people wrong as I chuckle at the thought. Is that bad? Sorry, not sorry. I honestly feel like nobody has the right to box people into what society or statistics say they should do and be. Everyone has the right to go as far in life as their mind, ambition, work ethic and skills allow them to go. I also celebrate on behalf of others whenever I see people winning, who weren't expected to, as their wins silence their doubters.

There are so many labels that could have discouraged me from trying most of the things I've accomplished, if I believed that those things had the power to do so. I was a second-generation teen mom, pregnant when I graduated from high school, had a trauma history (multiple layers), low self-esteem, quiet, shy, female, African American, grew up on the lower side of the middle class, just above the poverty line and lived below it at times. I had children by more than one man, I was divorced and remarried multiple times, bounced from toxic relationship to toxic relationship. All of these things that occurred throughout my life, the poor choices that I made, the mistakes, the lapses in judgement, and all of the labels could have kept me bound and unable to move forward. There are people who stood in critical judgement of me while I was experiencing these situations and those who still stand in judgement of me as if to hold me hostage to the past versions of myself. But I know who I am. I've grown and evolved so much as a person over the years that the reality is that the people who knew me back then, don't know me now, and the labels and boxes that they would use (if they were able) to keep me bound and stuck…I smashed through them a long time ago. There are people who won't allow you to evolve, in their minds, no matter how much success you achieve, you'll always be little "so and so" from down the street. They'll gossip about you, they'll say "Oh she used to…" in an attempt to strip away your confidence and essentially say "How dare you grow personally & professionally?" Let them talk, let them think how they think, and feel how they feel. Their thoughts and words only have power if YOU give them power. Again, I say, stay rooted in who you know yourself to be and keep your thoughts elevated.

There was a time when I worked for a large non-profit organization. I was a case manager for a youth program, which

was one of many community service-oriented programs provided
by this organization. In that role, I routinely felt underappreciated,
undervalued, and stepped on by those in positions of authority
and the ones who felt like they were in positions of authority. I
put in the work, I was great at connecting with the youth because
I was relatively young myself and I genuinely cared about the
program participants' successes. I saw myself in some of them.
They were primarily African American, came from disadvantaged
communities and situations and had made the decision to be a
part of this program for an opportunity to better their lives. In
addition to the ways that I continually went above and beyond
for the program participants I also completed the reporting for
the program which impacted the grant funding available. That
wasn't a part of my job. It was my manager's job, but I completed
the tasks he gave me and kept my mouth shut when he passed
my work along to the program director as if he'd completed the
work himself. In addition to that, there was the nicety (nice/nasty)
coordinator for the program who hated me from the moment she
set eyes on me. I understood why, I was young, and attractive, the
program participants liked me, I received compliments from other
colleagues, and she felt threatened by that. I just delved into my

work, doing the best I could do with the little resources provided
and tried to dodge any of the figurative bricks thrown at me. But as
good as I was in that role there was one person who never seemed
satisfied with my work. He seemed to make it his personal mission
to make sure I knew what level he saw me as being on. That was
the program director. He was a large, and burly man. He stood
at least 6'4", towering over most of us, in his ill-fitting suits and
doused in expensive cologne to the extent that you could smell
him coming. His scent or stench would also linger like a cloud of
arrogance long after he'd left the room. In all my life, still to this
day I've never encountered someone in a professional setting who
was so unhinged and unprofessional. In department meetings he
would yell, curse, slam things, beat on the table like King Kong,
shove things, belittle and intimidate. And I, a twenty something at
just over 5 feet tall and about 115lbs, was frequently the target or
scapegoat. Every minor oversight, or perceived slight was amplified
during these meetings. It got so bad that I began to have panic
attacks in the hours leading up to the scheduled meeting times.
Everything about him and his behaviors triggered me. As a young
woman, who was small in stature and a survivor of multiple kinds
of abuse and violence he was the antithesis to what would have

made that place a productive work environment. There were times I cried in the parking lot before going into the building. But it was a "good" job by many people's standards, steady pay (less than what I deserved) and benefits for me and my two young daughters. What I experienced, I felt I had no recourse, there was nobody I could report it to. I didn't feel that reporting it to HR or any other person in the organization would make a difference. The President/ CEO of at the time was the person this Program Director reported to, and she was essentially his "God Mother". This is how he was able to get away with this kind of behavior for so long, everyone knew that reporting it would do no good.

I continued to do what I needed to do to get my work done, in the midst of that toxic environment, all while praying that something would change. And in less than a year I was invited to apply for a role in Human Resources. There were changes happening within that program, layoffs were coming, and little did I know, there were conversations being held in rooms where someone had noticed my work, my skills and was advocating on my behalf. This person who advocated for the organization to keep me, by considering me for an HR opening, I credit her with shifting my life in a different direction. She came to me, told me to apply for the opening, it would be a position in HR which combined recruiting with the pre-hire and onboarding tasks for the organization. I was intrigued and thankful but responded that I didn't have any HR experience. She told me to apply anyway, I interviewed, got the job and was plucked out of that toxic program which freed me from being under the thumb of "King Kong".

I was so excited, I'd never considered Human Resources as a career, but I'm a fast learner and quickly fell in love with all things recruitment, workforce development, employee engagement, etc. This opportunity set the stage for a career that grew over the years and laid the foundation for my expertise in talent acquisition and human resources disciplines. And that expertise is what gave me the confidence to really monetize my skill set by starting my recruitment & staffing agency almost 8 years later.

(Boss Baby Camden, April 2021)

Chapter 5

The Process

"Keep your eyes on the stars, and your feet on the ground."

-Theodore Roosevelt

We have all heard the old adage that "a diamond is a lump of coal that handled pressure exceptionally well". Sorry to disappoint anyone who believed this to be factually correct. Diamonds do not come from lumps of coal. They are different substances that each originate under-ground, encounter extremely high temperatures and high pressure to form but they are not the same. Coal consists of carbon and dead plant matter; it also forms much closer to the earth's surface than diamonds. Another difference: diamonds consist purely of carbon minerals (a pure phase or polymorph of diamonds), subjected to high temperatures, high pressures and are found much further beneath the earth's surface than coal. So, the old adage, can be modified to focus on the fact that diamonds are created as a result of high pressure and heat they experience…leaving coal out of it entirely.

We know that the objective of the diamonds and coal quote

is meant to motivate individuals through difficult situations. There are challenges, disappointments and setbacks that occur through every stage of life. As you're growing and evolving into the person you were meant to be, elevating your life to the next level and/or growing your business, you will encounter ups and downs. It's a part of the process. You can't let fears of that process hinder you from moving forward or making efforts towards growth. One thing I've talked about in interviews and in motivational speeches I've given is that God will give you a vision that sparks your excitement, but he won't show you the path it'll take to get there. The reason for that is, if he showed you the road you'd have to take to get to that vision, you might get too afraid to move forward and take the first step. That road isn't smooth. It's raggedy, with fallen tree limbs, roadblocks, mountains, pits filled with quicksand and occasionally the need to take or create alternate routes. Even if you aren't religious, you get the gist of what I'm saying here. When you have an idea that inspires and lights a fire within you, it's the excitement that causes you to take action. But we know that if you could see ahead into what that journey would look like, there are likely to be challenges there that might have deterred you from ever getting started. The "Process" is necessary though. However daunting it can be to encounter the losses, perceived failures, mistakes and missteps, those things are meant to teach us and help to shape the end result.

Entrepreneurs know all too well that the road to success is filled with twists, turns and losses. Not everyone is meant to be a full-time entrepreneur though social media seems to scream at that it's the ideal, working for yourself, being your own boss. This idea focuses primarily on the pretty side of the coin when it comes to being entirely dependent on yourself to build and grow a business. The other side is until you've put in unlimited amounts of time, effort, resources and gone through the process of being told no more often than yes, living off of your savings as you work to build a client base and generate revenue, you haven't seen the ugly side of the coin. I came across a post recently that said "full-time entrepreneurs eat what they kill" which refers to the idea that unless you work, you don't get paid. There are also times when a great deal of work hours are put in and there isn't any immediate pay to follow. It's a shock to the system when you're accustomed to a steady paycheck that comes from a job working for someone else. Full time entrepreneurship requires a tenacity that most people don't have, and that's ok. There is nothing wrong with working for a living, working for a company, a person or organization. Don't let social media glamorize entrepreneurship to the extent that you choose it, only to end up disappointed. And it's entirely possible, to work a full-time job while having side businesses if you want to monetize your skills while maintaining the stability of a steady paycheck. Full time entrepreneurship is not for the faint of heart.

I mentioned the start of my recruitment & staffing agency in earlier chapters of this text, but I didn't share much about what the process looked like after I did it. Was there some success? Yes. But were there losses? Absolutely. Those things ultimately taught me about the business, it forced me to reevaluate what I knew, and had learned. I had to revamp my recruitment contracts and strategies multiple times. Each time I came across a "loss" or a scenario that didn't work out as expected, I took the loss and found the lesson. There were many times where I wanted to give up, I second guessed my decision, I felt I was doing everything I could to work my business and provide quality services with integrity. But there are people in the business world who aren't great client/ customers and will try to take advantage at every turn, especially if they have the impression that your business is newer. I had great success with a particular recruitment contract that I landed, it was my first one, and it built my confidence showing me that what I'd set out to do…could be done. Back to that idea of being shown the vision and but not the difficult road ahead, I believe that the initial success I found was God giving me a bit of encouragement to keep going. It galvanized me enough to put in the work and grind to attain other recruitment contracts, because since I'd successfully done it, I was confident that it would be "easy peasy", rinse & repeat. It wasn't. After my first contract, I secured other contracts, but it was loss after loss. Awful client companies with hiring managers that brought me on, just to syphon my time and resources but not pay me for my work. I even had to file a lawsuit against one of those companies. I'd mistakenly thought that in business, there was a level of integrity that was implied, and if you're providing services to legitimate businesses that there would be a level of legitimacy in their practices. There are sharks in the business world, just like there are in other corners of society, I encountered a few but I learned from those experiences. So why do I call this season "The Process"? Because the story doesn't end here. The losses I encountered, taught me more about myself and business than the wins. And though I ultimately decided to dissolve this particular business, I don't count it as a loss. My career experience in HR combined with the experience I gained running my own recruitment and staffing agency boosted my skill set and expertise to the next level. Which qualified me for talent acquisitions roles that paid more than double what I made in my previous HR role for the health department. This realization showed me that I have no desire to run a staffing agency or work any contingent hire recruitment contracts. I also realized that I dislike the business development side of "staffing-preneurship" (sourcing for client companies) and I'd rather focus on the recruitment & workforce development side of things.

The lesson in this is that it's ok to pivot if something you are doing isn't working for you. If you are bold enough to set out on an uncharted path, there's no way to predict how things will go even with the best in preparation. And no situation is ever a failure if it taught you something valuable. In this scenario, God simply used my recruitment & staffing firm as a vehicle to move me to the next level, it was never meant to be any more than that and I am grateful. The highs and lows, all of it was ultimately worth it to get me where I needed to be which is making double, then triple what I made in the HR role I left during the pandemic. That decision allowed me to work fully remotely, elevate my skills, and my life. If I'd stayed in that role I would have been waiting on 1-2% annual raises and living just above the poverty line. For even more context, the HR director at that health department had been working there for 20 years to get to the salary she was making. I surpassed that income in less than one year by leaving that role, running my firm and then dissolving my firm to be a freelance contract recruiter and HR consultant. Now I have the best of both worlds, I have the freedom of working for myself, fully remote, and the steady income of being a subcontractor who is paid an hourly rate at 40 hours per week. I invoice these companies for my work on a weekly basis. And to top it all off, the hourly rate I am paid, is more than I ever dreamt of making or asking for. Now, if ever I did decide to accept another internal HR or recruitment role, the requirement would be no less than a six-figure salary because it would have to be at minimum, what I'm making now as a freelancer.

Secure the B.A.G. if you know, you know. And in all things, use your best judgement and wisdom.

(Will & Cami become first time homebuyers June 2022)

Chapter 6

Intentionality

"Deciding what not to do is as important as deciding what to do."

-Steve Jobs

What does success look like for you? Get clear on what that means for YOUR life. It's different for everyone, there is no cookie cutter image or catch all for what success looks like and feels like for any of us. And whatever it looks like now, once you've reached it, the goal post moves, and the vision evolves.

Take some time to meditate on YOUR idea of success. Literally close your eyes and visualize it:

- What sounds do you hear, what do you see around you, what are you wearing, feeling?
- What things are in place in your life (personally & professionally)?
- Write those things down and/or create a vision board or folder of images that represent those things.

- Then define the goals, specific goals, short term and long term, along with 3 action steps you can take to start working towards them.

If you can picture your ideal self, this version of yourself that is successful. This version of yourself 5-10 years from now:

- What does that version of you look like, or sound like?

- What level of expertise does this version of you need to have in order to be living out your dream career?

- What are the personality characteristics that this version of you needs to have to reach this level of success?

Clarity is important. To just say you want to be successful but having no specific goals or idea of what that means for you isn't going to get you anywhere. And if you have ideas but are open to getting help to develop them, expound, and strategize, there is help available. I offer professional development coaching as a part of the services I provide through one of my businesses. Coaching can be a buzz word nowadays, there are lots of people offering "coaching" with no clear description of what that means, what you're paying for and how it will help you. The coaching I offer is very specific in the techniques used for clarifying your goals, strategizing (creating a plan or multiple plans of action), and then implementing the plan with deadlines, as well as resources to help.

We are truly in a magnificent age in time when there is so much money to be made and technology has put it all right at our fingertips. The fact that we can provide services to individuals or companies all over the world is awe inspiring. You can monetize your skills and hobbies. Maybe you have a skill set that's not being utilized at all or it's underutilized in your day-to-day career. There is a market for every skill set and a way to monetize it. It's just a matter of identifying what those skills are, researching the market, and strategizing. Will every idea end up turning into a multi-million-dollar enterprise? No, but those underutilized skills could certainly afford you some additional income, be leveraged for a higher paying salary, and/or free up time for other things in your life.

Now, on to what you don't want. It's necessary to be clear on what you don't want in order to stay focused on what you do want.

- That means saying no to anything that doesn't
  fit into the vision you have for your life, both
  personally and professionally.

- Developing the level of assertiveness that's required
  once you've reached a certain level of success. You
  can't be a push over, bending to everyone's whim
  and expectations, if you're a people pleaser by
  nature it takes time and intentionality to develop
  the ability to say "no" unapologetically. And "no"
  is a full sentence, so being able to say it without the
  guilt or feeling the need to overly explain why.

- Time is the one commodity you can never get back,
  use it wisely and don't waste it on things that aren't
  tied to your goals.

- Discernment, work on developing it and if you're
  like me, pray for it as you develop it. It can save
  you a lot of time and heart ache if you're able to
  use your wisdom and ability to assess as a way to
  weed out the people and opportunities that mean
  you no good. And in the non-religious sense, it's a
  tool for taking notice of the red flags in people, and

opportunities instead of excusing behaviors and explaining them away. There's a difference in giving people the benefit of the doubt and plainly ignoring the signs that a person or opportunity isn't on the up and up. This will always be key, personally and professionally. I could have avoided many of the toxic relationships I've encountered throughout my life were it not for me excusing and ignoring red flags as they revealed themselves. And, not just in romantic relationships, that's been the case in friendships and business relationships also.

- Valuing your time and your worth properly. If your business provides a service, and you know that you provide quality services, don't under value your offers. Don't be afraid to charge higher rates because you are afraid to not get clients/customers. There are services provided and available at every price point. Clients/customers who can't afford your rate aren't your target audience. For this reason, you need to be clear on who your target audience is. So many people waste their time marketing

products and services to the public with no regard
for who they really need to be targeting and
tailoring their approach to reach that particular set
of clients/customers. This is what I mean when I
say strategize. Don't wing it, don't do the spaghetti
method, and throw it all out there hoping something
will stick. You'll save yourself time and effort when
you are clear on your goals, who benefits most
from your products or services, where to find those
people, what kind of marketing will garner their
attention etc.

On the flip side of this, have the integrity to make sure you
are actually providing quality services. Nothing irritates me more
than seeing people market their products and posting "yesterday's
price isn't today's price", but what they're offering isn't up to par.
That to me is the same as scamming people out of their money.
You can't charge top dollar for what you do, if you suck. Sorry, not
sorry. You should constantly seek out ways to upgrade your skills
and what you provide if you are audacious enough to think raising
your prices on a regular basis is a valid move to make. Be open to
constructive criticism as well, seek out feedback on what you could

be doing better. It may get you a few dollars in the short term, not doing business with integrity but the best marketing is going to be the great reviews you get from your satisfied customers. Doing good work will always be the best way to continue building your brand and customer base.

(Cami Barnes, October 2022, Fox 5 Atlanta Studio

for Domestic Violence Awareness Interview)

Chapter 7
The Law of Attraction

"Happiness is not something readymade; it
comes from your own actions."

-Dalai Lama

Living life authentically and doing business with integrity
is the key to continually attracting good opportunities, and
resources into your life. Everything in life exists on a frequency
and you can decide to vibrate on a low frequency or a high
frequency, attracting the kinds of things you want based on the
frequency you operate on. If your mindset is constantly seeing
the negatives, speaking the negatives, you will continue to attract
negative things, people and situations into your life. Conversely
operating on a higher frequency, elevating your thoughts, positively
reframing what might be perceived as a negative to others,
making your vision plain, focusing on those higher-level things,
listening/repeating positive affirmations, you will attract high level
people, things and opportunities to your life. This is a simplified
explanation of the Law of Attraction, that's existed for thousands

of years. A similar concept is the idea of reaping and sowing, as referenced in the Bible and other religious texts.

You may ask yourself the question at times, if this is true, why is "so & so" (the bad person) seemingly doing well despite being awful, lacking integrity etc.? It's a question that the best of us have pondered at one time or another when we're encountering difficult seasons of our lives. We are human, we all have our moments when we're feeling down, or frustrated. It's how you navigate those feelings that makes all the difference. Feel the feelings but don't dwell there. Ask yourself what that situation is trying to teach you, what are the key takeaways? Flip that negative situation on its head and find a way to use it to your advantage. This is a way to keep yourself from spiraling down a negative thought loop and vibrating on a low level. It's not helpful to get to that place and stay there. Whenever you find yourself feeling out of sorts emotionally, feeling mentally drained, that's your cue to identify the problem or problems and start coming up with solutions. There is a solution to every problem, there may be choices that are more or less ideal than others, but those choices exist and you always have an option to make a different choice. You are never stuck, even if you feel that way. You aren't. Bouncing back from disappointments is a superpower, it conveys a strength and resilience. And if you don't have that ability, it's something you should be working and striving to develop. There will never be a complete absence of disappointments, sadness or frustration, these things are just a part of life, but you can choose not to let those things throw you completely off course. That's the biggest difference between someone who has emotional intelligence and someone who lacks it. And if you lack it, don't feel attacked by me pointing that out, get intentional about changing that, it's a skill that can and should be developed.

There are five characteristics of emotional intelligence:

- Self-Awareness- Do you know what your triggers are? When something upsets you are you able to do an internal assessment of why that thing, situation or person is causing this reaction in you?

- Self-Regulation- When you are triggered and recognize you've been triggered, are you able to see that situation for what it is and reel yourself back in emotionally? We all have histories, and things in our pasts that may trigger emotional responses in us when we feel we're encountering something similar or something that feels similar (even when it's not a similar situation at all). And it's normal to feel triggered, it's a human response that is meant to protect us but it's not always accurate so it's important to have the ability to rationally assess the situation and self-correct.

- Motivation- Do you have an internal drive or determination to get on track and stay on track? Or does everything fall by the wayside when you're not in a good space emotionally? You can and should take a break, rest, relax and utilize self-care tools when you need to, it's necessary. But it's important to be able to do that and maintain the motivation to get back to it and not lose focus. Take the moment, renew your mind, body and spirit then get back at it. Stay the course, keep your focus on your goals.

- Empathy- Do you have an awareness of other people's thoughts and feelings? Are you able to acknowledge other people's points of view without getting defensive? If not, work on that. It's important for your growth.

- Social Skills- Do you have a good grasp of effective communication skills? Can you express yourself, the good and the bad in a way that conveys what you want to say without it being offensive, harmful, hurtful, disrespectful, or mean spirited? It's much easier to communicate respectfully when you aren't triggered. And if you can't communicate effectively or respectfully when you are, take a moment to process and collect yourself before verbalizing your thoughts. Words can't be taken back once they've been said, and apologies, however well-intentioned can't rewind time or erase the memory as if it never occurred.

Work on these things as if the quality of your life depends on it, because it does. These are the tools for operating at a higher frequency and actively working to avoid low vibrational thoughts and behaviors. "As a man thinketh, so is he" Proverbs 23:7 comes to mind here. And "Thoughts become things", a quote by Bob Proctor. You can't attract what you're seeking if your thinking and mindset is flawed. We should always be striving to become the best version of ourselves to make the best use of our gifts and our time in this world. So, get your mind right, go forth and be great.

(Safe Space ATL receives a donation from the NFL

Alumni Georgia Chapter at the 4th Annual Holiday

Toy & Coat Drive Event in December 2022)

Chapter 8
Cutting off Dead Connections

"If people are doubting how far you can go, go
so far that you can't hear them anymore."

-Michele Ruiz

Why do we hold on to the ideas we have of people that
aren't based in the realities that they've shown us? I can think of
multiple instances of relationships and friendships lasting much
longer than they should have because of me trying to hold on to
an image I had of them or my connection to them. For people
you aren't related to, relationships are built over time and through
shared experiences. Those relationships grow and may consist
of positive examples to support continuing on with them (in
whatever capacity they exist in your life, romantically, platonically
or professionally). And there will be a peppering of negative
examples, or what you'll later call red flags, that you missed once
things finally hit a wall and you're done. Your heart can be in the
right place as you meet new people, bring them into your world,
and approach everything with only the best intentions but that

doesn't mean the other person has that same outlook. There are people with hidden agendas who will try to attach themselves to you for reasons beyond what they're willing to expose. Maybe they see your light, they see your capabilities, the way you approach things, the way people respond to you and want to latch on to that, hoping to get a piece of that by association. Or maybe they just want to align themselves to get whatever they can get from you, using manipulation tactics to make it seem as though their connection with you is going to benefit you in some way. There are people who will do this and interject themselves so firmly in your life that they have the access to sabotage you, in big ways and small ones. And then when you call them out on it, they'll get defensive and try to either make you feel guilty for doubting them or flip the situation on you to somehow make their actions or lack thereof your fault.

When you start to see these dynamics playing out, start mentally preparing to cut these folks off. It does you no good to let this go on for longer than necessary, as I mentioned before, wasted time is worse than wasted money because there will always be money to be made. Time, you can't get it back. You can't go to the time store and ask to buy another year, day, hour, etc. Once that time is gone, it's gone so don't waste it. When you see that a person isn't in alignment with where you see things going in your life, cut your losses, and cut them off. This goes for any type of relationship, family, romantic, platonic, and business. There are people who will try their best to hold on their connections with you, even when they see things aren't going well, and sometimes especially because things aren't going well, and they are upset about it. They aren't going to be willing to walk away without getting what they set out to get from you or without trying to leave you somehow worse off than when you started out with them. Beware of that especially, the slights and sabotage that will start to ensue once you've called someone out on something they've done or not done, and you decide to give them another chance. It almost always works out more in their favor than yours to give them another opportunity to disappoint you, because some of them will take offense to you bringing the behavior to their attention and begin to do things out of spite. My rule of thumb is, fool me once, shame on you, fool me twice, shame on me. There is no third time, by then, you're gone.

Familial relationships are trickier though. There's a level of loyalty and the benefit of the doubt that you can feel led to give to family members that you wouldn't give to anyone else. At all times use discernment and wisdom. When people show you who they are, believe them and deal with them accordingly. Learn from the bumps and bruises. With family, if you feel the situation doesn't rise to the level of cutting them out of your life completely, you can just establish firm boundaries and limit their access to you and your life. It's entirely possible to love someone, want the best for them but know that for your own peace of mind and prosperity you have to love them from a distance. And those family members you've distanced yourself from, when you see them, let it be all love, be cordial, love on them but let that be it. There's no need to be rude or disrespectful just because you've decided to change the boundaries and access to your life. Don't operate from a space of negativity that will harm your peace and mindset. Remember the previous chapter, the negative energies, actions, and thoughts you put out will invite those things into your life. You have too many great things to work on and accomplish, too many big ideas, dreams, and goals to not be actively working on keeping your thoughts and actions elevated.

In business, a tree is known by its fruit. If there's a tree on your team or in your life that isn't producing any fruit, it's not serving any relevant purpose. Let it go. And do so with the facts being on your side. As a leader, make sure expectations are clearly outlined, create a description of what this person's role entails, have them sign it when you bring them onboard. If they aren't producing or adhering to what they agreed to do as a part of that team, bring it to their attention and do it with empathy. Use your best judgement and if there are valid reasons for why something wasn't done or was done, document that too and provide them with coaching on what should be done instead. But if this behavior seems to be a pattern or larger problem, let them go and be clear on what the expectations were, how they didn't meet them and let the decision be based in fact, not emotion. People will get emotional when they feel slighted or rejected in some way. Even when the decisions are based in fact, mentally prepare for the fact that not everyone has the emotional intelligence (as outlined earlier in the text) to see the situation for what it is, business, not personal. Make the decision and do so without second guessing your decision or overthinking it. If the person you've decided to eliminate from your team decides to take the decision personally and responds poorly, don't take it personally, even if they try to attack you personally. Their feelings are a "them" problem. You did your part in the beginning, by outlining the expectations that they agreed

to. Everything else is a moot point, so stand on that. The facts will

always be the facts. What's in black in white? What did they sign?

Okay? Make the decision and leave it there.

(Cami & Baby Camden, Promoting Linked4Launch.com 2022)

Chapter 9
Be Coachable

"Smart people learn from everything & everyone, average people from their experiences, stupid people already have all the answers"

-Socrates

There is nobody walking the earth who knows everything there is to know about everything. There are experts in every field, but even those who know more than most people can still learn new things. Don't ever be so rigid in your thinking that you assume that you've reached a level of success that there's nothing new to be revealed to you through insightful conversations, coaching and or shifts in perspective. One of our goals should be to find a lesson in everything and to have a desire to expand our thinking so that we can tap into an influx of new ideas and innovation.

If you are a builder or inventor working on a project and you encounter a problem, but you aren't satisfied with the solutions you usually implement to solve this problem. And you continue staring at this project, going over and over your plans, again and again but can't seem to find a different solution, the answer is to bring in someone who can look at the project from a different perspective. At this point, you're too close to the problem, it's harder for you to see beyond the problem itself, what you'd envisioned for the project, and your go-to solutions that you've used in the past. Someone coming in with a fresh viewpoint of the project, the problem and other possible solutions could be just what's needed to get the project back on track and elevate it to the next level. This is why coaching works. There are so many times in life when we've encountered challenges, overcome them, had successes and think, ok I've made it here, I've accomplished this goal...now what? Then we establish new goals and get to work on those only to find that the methods we took to reach the previous goals aren't quite doing the job to get us through to the next phase of success. A professional development coach can help you to find clarity, provide a new perspective, with fresh ideas, solutions and assist in creating a strategic plan for implementing those solutions. You should never feel stuck, as I mentioned before in this text, there is a solution for every problem. Sometimes that "stuck" feeling is just in our heads because we can't see beyond the problem that's in front of us, so we just need someone to come in and shift our view in a different direction. Even coaches have coaches. Your favorite speakers, mentors, coaches, and other successful people have other people who they bounce ideas off of, who they talk through their challenges with to find the right solutions to get them over the proverbial hump. But not everyone, especially those who are up and coming, has likeminded people to do this with. You won't get the same results talking to just anyone who will listen, though you can find wisdom and learn from everyone and everything. When it comes to strategic thinking and accomplishing specific goals a coaching session is what will help you to get there.

There was a time when someone I truly cared about didn't seem to value my input, advice or ideas. This person would encounter challenges or would be doing things in a certain way, I'd see a more efficient solution and suggest it to them. Any input I gave was met with dismissal, and occasionally the person would even take offense to my suggestions because they felt like since they'd had "x" number of years working in that industry. In their mind, they were the expert so who was I to tell them anything? The irony in all of this is that the same person would later come to me and say that "so and so" told me I should do "x,y,z" (the same advice I'd given them), and somehow the information was valid coming from that other person. When I'd point it out, that this advice was the same advice I'd given, again…I was met with a dismissive attitude.

Value the resources that you have available to you. There may be people that you're connected to who don't work in your industry but could be tied to an idea or another person that could catapult you to the next level. Humility is a superpower. Being humble enough to be coachable allows you to tap in and really receive the blessings you're meant to have. No matter what level of success you've reached, keep your feet on the ground and stay flexible in your thinking. Don't ever get to a point of being so comfortable and complacent that you stop growing and learning.

(Cami & Will modeling Power Couple t-shirts designed

by gohardcustoms.com, November 2022)

Chapter 10

Manifesting

"Go confidently in the direction of your dreams.

Live the life you have imagined."

-Henry David Thoreau

There are people on social media who have the wrong idea about what it means to manifest the life you've dreamed of. Lately I've seen instances of people thinking that manifesting is about replacing God and prayer. I've also read statuses on Facebook that are only focused on the "speaking things into existence" part of manifesting. Both of these are wrong. So for the religious folks among us, you aren't sinning by using the term manifest, or any variation of it when it comes to accomplishing your goals. In fact, prayer can certainly contribute to the manifestations of what you want to accomplish in your life. It all starts with a vision, you see this goal or this thing that you want to do in your mind, you picture it. But in order to manifest it, you have to put work and strategy behind that vision in addition to the prayer, positive affirmations etc. The law of attraction focuses on your training your mind to be able to attract those positive things that you want into your life by elevating your thoughts. And if you are religious, a Christian specifically, you should be familiar with the idea that "faith without works is dead". You can have all the faith in the world, you can pray and fast, and read every version of the bible but if you aren't putting forth any actual effort towards accomplishing that goal, it's unlikely to happen. Nobody is going to come and knock on your door to give your heart's desire to you. Be clear about what it is that you want, have a vision, make it plain, write it down, create a plan (or if you're like me, multiple plans), research, educate yourself and implement your plan along with having the faith, the prayers and the visualizations. It is entirely possible to manifest your dreams if you are doing everything possible to put yourself in position to have those things that you dream of. Whether it's a healthy relationship, career satisfaction, etc.

- If what you want to manifest is related to a romantic relationship, the first thing you should do is get clear on what you do want and what you don't want in a mate.
- What are YOUR deal breakers?
- What are you willing to compromise on?

- Are you open to the possibility that what you're looking for may not look like what you imagined?

- Are you actively working on yourself?

- Are you willing to go to therapy to heal from past traumas and learn new ways of coping and communicating? You want to go into your next relationship as a better person who is continually striving to be better. And as a WHOLE person, not half of a whole. Broken-ness, un-healed trauma is like a magnet for the same person in a different body to keep showing up in your life. Lessons will repeat until you learn from them. Break the cycle.

- Are you working on elevating your life, physical health and finances? Don't be a man or a woman inviting someone to your struggle. There is nothing good about an invite to the struggle. If you are struggling in any area, focus on getting your life on track before you start dating. It's not fair to anyone to be burdened with fixing your problems, that's for you to do.

- This person you're looking for, what kind of interests do they have? Where might you meet that person? Join some professional networking groups, attend professional events, and other events that are specific to some of the characteristics you're looking for in a potential mate. You aren't likely to find that person at the grocery store. And if you're not interested in the party life and past your prime, it's just as unlikely that you'll find them at your local night club or bar. In order to get something you've never had, you have to be willing to do something you've never done. Think outside the box.

For your career:

- What are the qualifications or skill set needed for your ideal role?

- Are there specific education requirements, certifications, trainings that would provide you with the skill set needed to get to that level?

- What is the length of time that it could take for you to attain the expertise or education required?

- Are you willing to put in the work which may include taking a lower-level role that's on the trajectory to getting to that higher level role?

- What are the characteristics that a person in that role and with that title should have? Who do YOU have to become to transform into this person that YOU have dreamt of being.
- Research the answers to the questions above, put together a plan, give yourself deadlines and get to work!

Nobody is going to just hand you anything, you have to do the work, there's no way around it. That work is a part of the process to prepare and qualify you for what you're saying you want. Now…that…ladies and gentle folk, is manifestation. You honor God and you honor yourself by utilizing the brain you have, your skills, your resourcefulness and your wisdom to become the best possible version of yourself. That is what will put you in a position to receive all that you've ever wanted to have.

(Cami & Daughters at the Inaugural Thrive

Fundraising Gala for Safe Space ATL, October

2022, photo credit: Tara Harp Photography)

Chapter 11
Gratitude

"Be thankful for what you have; you'll end up having more. If you focus on what you don't have, you will never, ever have enough."

-Oprah Winfrey

What if I shared with you that gratitude is the key to unlocking new levels in your life? Being grateful can completely shift your mindset from negative to positive, no matter what's happening in your life. And that is the ultimate key to attracting and manifesting what you truly desire. It all ties in directly to the law of attraction and keeping your thoughts elevated. Challenges will happen, there will be rough times and situations that occur in your life but it's how you choose to respond to those things that will dictate what happens next. No matter how bad a situation appears, things could always be worse. There is ALWAYS something that you can take away from any situation and positively re-frame it by being grateful for what you do have because there are many people who don't have what you do, even if you don't have much.

- Don't have a flashy car right now? There are many people who don't have cars at all or any sort of reliable transportation.

- Don't have transportation? There are people who don't have the ability to walk or move around freely and/or without pain.

- Down to your last dollar? There are people who have been starving consistently and for extended periods of time and don't even have access to the basics like clean drinking water.

- You woke up to bad news? There are some who didn't wake up this morning and won't have the opportunity to make changes or regroup from whatever the situation is because they are gone.

There will ALWAYS be things happening that can put us in a bad mental space, but the key to emotional intelligence as I discussed earlier in this text is being able to recover quickly and pivot. It's a skill that not everyone has but I believe that everyone can acquire this skill if they practice it and are intentional about it. Challenges can make you better if you are willing to see the lesson in what's happening, shift your perspective to elevate your thoughts and focus on the solutions to the issue. Your first thought whenever a problem presents itself should be "what are the solutions to this problem?" Get solution focused, being too focused on the problem won't get you anywhere but stuck in the proverbial weeds. Don't spiral into a negative thought loop. Take a breath, identify the specific problem or problems in the situation, get a pen and paper if you must, and come up with three options or possible solutions for each issue. And after you've done that, verbalize what you are grateful for in that moment. Speak it out loud. Repeat the things you are grateful for, if necessary, to drown out any negative thoughts that are trying to take hold of you and keep you from moving forward. Listen to positive affirmations on repeat or empowering music on repeat if you must, in order to get your mind right. Unplug from distractions, pray, get outside, get some fresh air, in nature, meditate and do whatever YOU need to do to get your thoughts back on the right track and without delay. This should be an immediate response to what's happening so that you can get back to functioning at the level you're accustomed to. Don't let a hiccup in your plans ruin your entire morning, day or week. Take that individual situation for what it is and move on! Wasted time is worse than wasted money, (another thing I mentioned in earlier chapters of this text) and dwelling too long on an issue without working on solutions is a huge waste of time and energy. It'll leave you drained and can completely zap your motivation if you dwell in that frame of mind for too long. Shake it off, get yourself together and get to work on those solutions. Also, the solution may require hard conversations or choices on your part. You MUST get to the point where you are willing to prioritize your sanity, peace, wellbeing, and prosperity over the feelings of whoever might be negatively impacted by your conversation or decision.

- If the solution to an issue or frustration you're having is to have a discussion with someone about what they are doing to create these feelings in you, so be it. You have to be willing to say what needs to be said to honor yourself and your feelings.

- If the solution to the issue or frustration is to cut someone off, sever a business relationship, friendship, romantic relationship or going no contact with certain family members, you have to be willing to do that.

- If the solution is to leave a job you hate to pursue a goal or dream you have, you need to create an escape plan, start applying for other roles, start saving your money and have a set expectation for what you'll need to have in place in order to make the leap.

Life is too short to live it being miserable, stressed and not operating at the level that you know you're capable of. Eliminate what isn't working for you, when things don't go your way or the path you've chosen gets bumpy, identify what's creating the issue, strategize, make a move and shift your focus to the things you're grateful for as you navigate through it.

(Cami Barnes, January 2023, photo credit:

Dream Lens Photography)

Chapter 12

Stay Ready

"Success is where preparation and opportunity meet."

-Bobby Unser

One of the things that I struggled with for a good chunk of my life is anxiety. It's a very common issue particularly with high performers, people with trauma histories or people who fall into both categories like me. But I'm happy to report that I've turned this affliction into a strength by making it work for me in a way that helps me to stay on top of my game. How…might you ask did I conquer being anxiety prone? Well, it's with preparation. I am an over preparer. Having multiple options, and plans in place helps to quell any feelings of anxiousness in me. It's like a knee jerk reaction that if something is bothering me, I create plans. At any given point I'll have a plan A, B, C, D, E, F and G. Picture the little anxiety voice in your head poking and prodding you with the "what ifs", well I try to have an answer for each of those questions to essentially tell that voice to shut up and let me be great. It's much less likely that you'll talk yourself out of pursuing a goal, a path or whatever the idea may be if you've carefully considered the possibilities and are able to answer each of the "what ifs" with a possible solution, a way to pivot or an escape hatch. I'm so much of a preparer that I have literal nightmares of not being prepared, so I don't allow that in my conscious world if at all possible. And whenever spontaneous situations happen, my go to response is always to breathe, identify the issue, and identify options. So, even in the rare occasion that I'm not prepared for something, I'm usually able to keep a cool head, and think logically to keep from unraveling.

In addition to the anxiety relieving benefits, being prepared can also send a signal out to the world, to God and the Universe that you are ready to receive what you've said you wanted. Think of how it might feel to have someone approach you with an opportunity that you have to accept quickly or miss out, but you aren't prepared for it. That would be a tragedy. Therefore, if there is something you truly want, it's a MUST that you start preparing yourself to receive it. Whatever "it" is. That career you want, that relationship, whatever the case may be. That's why it's so important to think strategically and plan once you've clarified a particular goal. Having a plan of action is like flipping the light switch on the possibilities and saying, "okay let's do this". At that point you should be making the moves that'll get you closer to your goals and putting you in a position to receive the opportunity when it's presented to you.

If you have a business in a particular niche, you know your target audience, and there are events you can attend to connect with the right people, the first step is laying the foundation with preparation. Establishing the legitimacy of your business, your expertise, your products and services. Registering your business, your domain name, website, marketing materials etc. Even if you hadn't planned on attending an event right away, once you've flipped that light switch and put it out there in the atmosphere that this is what you're doing, opportunities can come your way at any time. And you have to be ready or miss out on them. One of my favorite sayings is "if you stay ready, you don't have to get ready", make sure you have what you need to be able to present the information about your business at any time. Be prepared to talk about your goods or services any time, and anywhere. There's no limit on the possibilities of where you might meet a potential customer, client or someone who could help you to take your business to the next level. There's not much that's worse than missed opportunities. But should you happen to miss one opportunity, don't get down in the dumps, take the lesson and do better the next time a similar opportunity presents itself.

(Cami Barnes, January 2023, photo credit:

Dream Lens Photography)

Final Thoughts

"We must believe that we are gifted for something and that this thing at whatever cost, must be attained." -Marie Curie

Now is the time to go boldly in the direction of your dreams. Don't keep putting your goals on the back burner, waiting for the perfect time to make a move. If you do that, the perfect time will never come, and years will have passed when you could have started today. I know that it can feel overwhelming if the goal is big enough and all you can see is the magnitude of it. If that goal is big enough it can make you feel too small to reach it, but you have to push past those feelings, and drown out the doubts. Whenever something feels too big for you to be able to handle, the best course of action is to break it down into smaller pieces so that it doesn't look so intimidating, and you can see it from a different perspective. Desmond Tutu once said, "There is only one way to eat an elephant; a bite at a time." If you can break that big goal or big thing down into smaller pieces, it's easier to snap out of those feelings of being afraid to get started. That's where your plan comes into play. You can do this. You can set those big, audacious goals, get clear on what success in those things look like for you, do the research, create a plan, and get to work on them. Wherever you are, I'll be here on the sidelines cheering you on and congratulating you every step of the way. I've even got a bonus for you; I've added a modified version of my workbook to the end of this text as a way to help jump start you on your journey. Use the workbook pages as a framework and benchmark you'll always be able to come back to it and see how far you've come. After you've filled these workbook and journal pages, get a new journal, and keep going. You can use the information over and over again, adapting and modifying as the goal post changes and you elevate to each level of success. And if you ever want to reach me directly, I'm pretty easy to find, you can book coaching sessions with me via my website www.CamiBarnes.com . I'd also like to invite you to join my Facebook group of goal getters, just search the book name to find the group. I hope to see and hear from you soon.

All the best,

Cami Barnes

(Cami Barnes, January 2023, photo credit:

Dream Lens Photography)

About the Author

Cami Barnes is a wife, mom, Atlanta businesswoman and a John Maxwell Program certified motivational speaker and leadership development coach.

She's overcome many obstacles and challenges in her life which includes being an abuse survivor and a second-generation teen mom who went on to become the first in her immediate family to graduate from college. Her experiences as a survivor inspired her to start Safe Space Property Management Inc, a 501c3 nonprofit organization that provides supportive services to survivors and domestic violence awareness education to the community. She is also the owner & operator of the job board www. Linked4Launch.com.

She has a career background in workforce development, human resources, mental health, social work and wellness. But it's her passion for inspiring and empowering others that keeps her centered. She's smashed through several barriers in her life and now she uses her platform to motivate others live out their dreams with courage and intention.

Securing the B.A.G (Big Audacious Goals)

Bonus Workbook

Date:

Writing Prompt

WEEK 1

What is does your ideal life look like, (family, career, financial, physical, spiritual)?
Visualize it and write it out:

_____

_____

_____

_____

_____

_____

_____

_____

_____

_____

_____

_____

_____

_____

_____

_____

_____

_____

_____

_____

_____

_____

Securing the B.A.G. Week 1

Goal for this week!

**Idea Dump zone
(to deal with later)**

3 Action Steps

1. ....
....

2. ....
....

3. ....
....

Notes:

3 Deadlines

1. ....
....

2. ....
....

3. ....
....

A note from Cami: "You
deserve all of the
amazing things that are
coming your way."

SHOW UP FOR YOURSELF THE WAY YOU SHOW UP FOR OTHERS!

Smart Goals

Setting realistic and achievable outcomes.

My biggest for this year is:

S SPECIFIC

What do I want to happen?	

M MEASUREABLE

How will I know when I have achieved this goal?	

A ATTAINABLE

Is the goal realistic & what are the steps I need to take to get started?	

R RELEVANT

Why is this goal important to me?	

T TIMELY

What is my deadline for this goal?	

Writing Prompt

WEEK 2

What are some potential challenges you may face on the journey towards manifesting the vision for your life? Think about it, write it out and then think of actions you can take to counter act those potential challenges.

_____

_____

_____

_____

_____

_____

_____

_____

_____

_____

_____

_____

_____

_____

_____

_____

_____

_____

_____

_____

_____

_____

_____

_____

Securing the B.A.G. Week 2

Goal for this week!

Idea Dump zone
(to deal with later)

3 Action Steps

1. ....
....

2. ....
....

3. ....
....

Notes:

3 Deadlines

1. ....
....

2. ....
....

3. ....
....

A note from Cami:
"Be bold enough to
go after everything
that you deserve!"

SHOW UP FOR YOURSELF THE WAY YOU SHOW UP FOR OTHERS!

Negative → Positive

Think about negative thought you had this week that you were able to positively reframe and describe it.

_____

_____

What prompted that thought?

_____

_____

_____

_____

_____

_____

Evidence against that thought:

_____

_____

_____

_____

_____

_____

Describe the positive version of the thought.

_____

_____

_____

_____

Writing Prompt

WEEK 3

Imagine that you traveled 10 years into the future and encountered yourself. You're 10 years older, your significant other and/or children are also 10 years older. You've achieved all of the goals that you had, you're happy and fulfilled. List some of the accomplishments you've achieved.

Securing the B.A.G. Week 3

Goal for this week!

Idea Dump zone
(to deal with later)

3 Action Steps

1. ....
....

2. ....
....

3. ....
....

Notes:

3 Deadlines

1. ....
....

2. ....
....

3. ....
....

<u>A note from Cami</u>: "There
is a past version of you
that is so proud of who you
are becoming. Keep going!"

SHOW UP FOR YOURSELF THE WAY YOU SHOW UP FOR OTHERS!

My Resilience Plan

Who can I share my thoughts & feelings with?

- _____
- _____
- _____

Ways for me to practice self care:

_____
_____
_____
_____

Three Things I'm Good At:

1 _____
2 _____
3 _____

A situation I've overcome:

_____
_____
_____
_____
_____

Ways to monetize my skills:

_____
_____
_____
_____
_____
_____
_____

Writing Prompt

WEEK 4

What resources or opportunities are being unused or underused in your life? What are some ways that you can improve your existing skills & talents? What impact would this have on your life?

_____

_____

_____

_____

_____

_____

_____

_____

_____

_____

_____

_____

_____

_____

_____

_____

_____

_____

_____

_____

_____

Securing the B.A.G. Week 4

Goal for this week!

Idea Dump zone
(to deal with later)

3 Action Steps

1. ....
....

2. ....
....

3. ....
....

Notes:

3 Deadlines

1. ....
....

2. ....
....

3. ....
....

<u>A note from Cami:</u> "There are
people who you haven't met
yet who will be impacted by
the person you are becoming."

SHOW UP FOR YOURSELF THE WAY YOU SHOW UP FOR OTHERS!

Challenges will come, get ready!

You can stay on track by being prepared. Create a self care tool kit to help you to push through the challenging days.

Music	A song that reminds you of a good memory.	A song that makes you feel pumped up.	A song that you'd listen to fall asleep.
Comfort Items Find 3 comfort items that help you to feel relaxed or at ease.	Item 1:	Item 2:	Item 3:
Places List 3 places you can go that can help you to relax & regroup.	Location 1:	Location 2:	Location 3:

Positive Affirmations

I'm excited to announce that I have items that I'm working on. I'll be sharing specifics in the Facebook group and via the website soon.

Subscribe and stay tuned for more!

- A mobile app
- An Audio Book of Guided Meditation

Thank you so much for being a part of my tribe!

Cami Barnes

Printed in the United States
by Baker & Taylor Publisher Services